Unacknowledged Legislations

Unacknowledged Legislations

Steve Henn

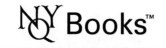

The New York Quarterly Foundation, Inc.
New York, New York

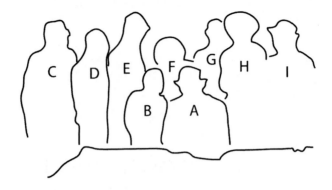

A. The President of the Disunited Statements of Bardic Manifestos
B. Zaya Henn—eldest daughter/inspiration
C. Dave Thompson—Poetry All Star/photographer/awesome shirt-wearer
D. Unky Steve Hively— Invisible Robot/confidante
E. Nate White- mouthharpist/cohomebrewer/Invisible Robot
F. Chris Foster—colleague/mentor
G. Ken Janda—as proxy for his brother, He Whom the Ladies Love
H. Kaveh Akbar—young punk/Poetry All Star/short order cook
I. Oren Wagner—Poetry All Star/godfather/tweeting savant

NYQ Books™ is an imprint of The New York Quarterly Foundation, Inc.

The New York Quarterly Foundation, Inc.
P. O. Box 2015
Old Chelsea Station
New York, NY 10113

www.nyqbooks.org

First Edition

Set in New Baskerville typeface.

Layout and Design by Raymond P. Hammond
Cover Photo by Lydia Henn

Library of Congress Control Number: 2010941897

ISBN: 978-1-935520-24-5

for Jack Musgrave
thank you, Jack

Acknowledgments

Some of these poems previously appeared in the following chapbooks:

The Seedy Underbelly of the Highfalutin' Oversoul
Platonic 3way Press, 2007

The 30th Anniversary Warsaw Community Commemorative Book Burning
Pudding House Publications, 2007

Subvert the Dominant Paradigm!
Boneworld Publishing/Musclehead Press, 2009

The Book of Nate
Superiority Complex Press, 2010

Showstoppers: 20 Poems from the Midwest Poetry All Stars
Superiority Complex Press, 2010

and on the audio CD:

Massacring the Laugh Track Audience, with musical accompaniment by
Rocket Surgeons, Doublestout Recordings, 2008

Thanks to the editors of the following magazines, where many of these
poems appeared:

*Quercus Review, Zen Baby, Chiron Review, New York Quarterly, 5AM, Fuck!,
Abbey, Freeverse, Barbaric Yawp, Hazmat Review, Staplegun, Pearl, Curbside
Review, www.ghotimag.com*

The Author would like to point out that all people and places mentioned
in this book are not the people and places of real life and/or actual his-
tory, but rather, people and places with their own special existence within
his imagination, even if they share names with others, including but not
limited to: "Charles Bukowski," "General Peter Pace," "Billy Sunday," "Abu
Graib," "I," "students," and "Warsaw, Indiana." The author notes that the
Billy Sunday that takes the place of Moloch in his homage to Ginsberg is
probably in many ways nothing like the Billy Sunday of actual history. And
that he is a big fan of the place where he grew up, and still resides.

Steve Henn would like to thank his friends and family, and especially the poets Oren Wagner, Don Winter, Kaveh Akbar, and David Thompson, for their continued camaraderie, encouragement, and support.

May God have Mercy on us all.

Table of Contents

III. Faith

IV. Sexuality

V. *after* **Ginsberg**

(Sigh) / 75

VI. Third Person

VII. First Person

Foreword

I just found out I have an ulcer. As compensation for my pound'f blood and enduring the purgatorial hospital waiting room, I received prescriptions for a couple opioid medications that, even when taken responsibly, turned a week of potentially mind-searing pain into a pretty relaxed half-remembered spell of hanging out in my underwear and eating Popsicles like I was getting paid by the stick.

Liberating as that sounds, hiding out in opiodic bliss is not at all conducive to the writing of intelligible prose. It's not conducive to the reading of intelligible prose. It's not even conducive to saying the word "intelligible." Its sole utility, really, is in facilitating euphoric napping.

That pretty succinctly establishes my view on the vast majority of poetry being published today. It exists, it's calming, and it almost always sounds like somebody's reading it on a radio fifty yards down the beach. But shit, life is not a beach (haw). You know what happens when you run along the noon surf in real life? You find out you have a fucking ulcer and start puking in the sand. It sucks. And then, when the drugs wear off, it's not breezy Balearic white noise fifty yards down the beach, but bright lights, sterile metal and a fat male nurse named Lenny humming Motley Crue's "Shout at the Devil" as he lubes up your catheter.

That's reality, though. Imperfect cacophony for our imperfect anatomies. Twenty-first century anxiety is born out of a collective human psychology evolving for tens of thousands of years to enable us as hunter-gatherers, then in the past century being thrust into a predominantly sedentary, increasingly impersonal world.

It is an anxiety that Steve Henn has battled his entire adult life, and one that informs most of his work. Today it is useless to be a creative thinker unless you can sell yourself along with your ideas, but Steve still elects to shoulder the Herculean task of being the singular provider for a family of six while attempting to produce a significant body of artifice —a body that lends amplification to the aesthetic soul trapped in a station marked by indifference (or open hostility) to such spirits.

In a world where the only safeguard of order and discipline is to construct populations of workers with interchangeable parts, Steve's work mocks, sneers, and laughs at those forces conspiring against his complete autonomy. He offers a singular breed of honesty bent by human isolation and captured in the poetic desire to communicate experience. He asks the reader to do the impossible, "drive away / unless the Truth has already killed you." The beach will still be there for less honest poets— the soundtrack to this drive is supremely, ferociously human.

—Kaveh Akbar

Poets are the unacknowledged legislators of the world.
—Percy Bysshe Shelley

If you want a picture of the future,
imagine a boot stomping on a human face—forever.
—Obrien, 1984

If you want me again look for me under your boot-soles
—Walt Whitman

I. Politics

There is nothing either good or bad but thinking makes it so.
—Hamlet

Come Live on My Commune!

It'll be out in a cornfield in Kosciusko County, Indiana,
where the wild marijuana grows!
We'll learn to make PCP from corn like this kid in high school
told me he could, and then we'll lift cars off trapped babies
and run marathons after getting shot in the leg and switch ourselves
with nettles and cut ourselves with broken beer bottles,
because *it doesn't hurt at all!*
We'll kidnap cows from nearby fields and free them
from the repressive practice of chewing cud!
We'll develop a breakthrough form of sexual intercourse
that consists of folk music, rubber bands, making oneself
cross-eyed, and armpit noises! We'll field trip
to Winona Lake Park and hold group therapy sessions
where you'll be considered eternally enlightened
if you can catch a duck with your bare hands!
We will smack you in the nipple! We will venerate
the third nipple as if it were a third eye! We'll blind
your third eye by spraying it with milk from our third nipples!
Men will take hormones so they can do this!
We will play Broadway show records backwards
on an old Victrola, uncovering subliminal messages
from Gay Satan! We will eat of the corn that grows
in the fields and poop out the corn to fertilize
the marijuana! When the cops show up and ask
who are you? what are you doing? we'll say
what are you doing, man? who are you, brother?
And if the cop's a chick we'll call her sister!
And if she gets out her pepper spray we'll go
really, sister, who are you? do you know who you are?
And she'll go *I'm an officer of the law,* and we'll go
no man, I mean sister, that's not who you are.
who are you, really? do you know who you are?
And the next thing you know she'll be doing
interpretive hippie dances among the kidnapped cows!
And Tim Leary and Ken Kesey and Hunter Thompson
and Janis Joplin and all those sixties saints
will descend from the clouds, and go,
hey man, show us that sex thing you do
with the rubber bands and crossed eyes and armpit noises
and stuff, that is way-out, daddy.

7 Layers of Irony Like the (In)famous Salad

First become a famous poet in spite of
all your desires to stay true
to the street or the working class or the People
or whatever you call the real deal where you come from
(around here it's all mixed up
in cornfields and basketball).
Then write about being a famous poet and hating it,
hating all the posers and their various attitudes.
Then juxtapose. As a Christian Atheist
or a Theistic Communist or a flaming straight man.
Emphatically deny the world
the synthesis of your thesis and antithesis. I mean
if you juxtaposed as a flaming straight man,
deny the existence of man-on-man sex, two-person comedy,
and things on fire. Add crumbled bacon.
Mix with not too much mayonnaise.
Allude to Brautigan. Throw
the whole damn thing out the window
of a moving train, into fields of lettuce
and arugula.

Why I'll Never Be an Artist

Because these things I do
are not as serious as death.
Because I dream, not
of writing the Great American Novel
but of winning the lottery
and living it up. Because I could never
starve for writing, and certainly
never cease drinking for it.
Because I am erratic, uninspired,
and unwilling to test my own boundaries.
Because providing for my family
holds precedence over any other sort
of integrity. Because I am unsure
of my ability. Because I do not
alienate the people I love in favor
of some higher ideal. Because
I would rather live a charmed life
than a tortured one.

Philosophers' Symposium on Animal Rights: "The Cow: Subject or Object?"

Attempting to settle the question with finality,
Do animals have rights? a gathering of national philosophers
and ethicists took up the question: the cow, subject or object?
at a C-SPAN-televised roundtable discussion. While some contended
that the cow is definitely an object, a four-legged conglomeration of beef
and beef-related articles, others were more generous. "Is it a pet cow?"
one eminent philosopher asked. A tangential discussion
of whether pet cows existed ensued, and after an impasse, the panel
determined that if a pet, a cow may be a subject,
granting it the right (like a dog) not to be killed
unless medical expenses became too much for the caretaker
to bear. Others noted that dairy cows, whether subject
or object, had a better life than the average female human,
who doesn't get her teats massaged or expressed
nearly as much as is reproductively and physically healthy.
They reached no final conclusion despite the exhortations
of a PETA agitator in the audience screaming, "Cows are people too!"
wearing a shirt reading, "If you prick them, do they not moo?"
and attempting to throw a shepherd's pie in the face
of the most vociferously pro-object panelist. The discussion
degenerated into a string theory–like mess
of hypotheticals and abstraction when mired in the issue
of the Ubercow: the cow who develops a supercow
intelligence and therefore is bound no longer by the physical,
emotional, or moral chains that have subjugated the species
for centuries. Indeed, the very raising of the issue
created such a hubbub that a S.W.A.T. team was called in
to tear-gas the convention center. No animals were injured
in the evacuation of the facility.

Democrat Sighting Reported in Kosciusko County

High-level government meteorological and paranormal
investigations officials are at a loss to explain
the Democrat sighting reported in Kosciusko County, Indiana,
on a county road next to a country church with a sign reading
GOD HATES SODOMITES AND FEMINISTS.
The unidentified liberal object was reportedly hailing passing cars
to hand out thank-you notes to women, homosexuals,
Native Americans, and other minorities for putting up with
male white corporate oppression and the resulting lack
of fresh vegetables in their diets all these years.
Reportedly, said object had thank-you's for a cryptic demographic
he called "African American" (we think he meant the Negroes),
none of whom could be located on the road, nor anywhere else
in the county at the time of this report. The Democrat has been
relocated to one of the cow stalls at the county fairgrounds
in the county seat, where, at first, he resisted
Republican directives to poop on the floor and find what
nutritional value he can in the stuff that grows on our lawns.
He misunderstood this rudimentary attempt at communication
to be a reference to something you smoke, whereas Republican
officials referred to the proferred foodstuff by the local term,
grass. The Democrat seems to be slowly slipping from sanity
as he continues to be alienated from his mother country;
more recent contact and observations include a gnashing of teeth,
repeated, near-hysterical pleas for something called "soy milk,"
and a sing-song muttering of snatches of "We Are The World."
The Democrat will be kept under observation, chained next to
a comfortable spot in the hay, until further notice.

A Virtual Tour of Brass Tacks Supermarket

Just inside the automatic doors sit the big bins
of Shit We Couldn't Sell Full Price That's Almost Expired.
Turn to the right. Walk through Our Attempt
to Put Your Local Florist Out of Business—you'll be standing
In front of Food You're Too Lazy to Heat Yourself.
Walk straight back through Horrendously Marked-up Produce
and by Baked Shit That Will Kill You and order
a choice cut of anything from the Cow Carcass and Soylent Green Counter.
Travel the length of the back—
on your right are Heavily Preserved Carcinogenic Meats
and Biogenetically Fucked-with Dairy Products. On your left
are the aisles labeled Stuff in Cans, Stuff in Boxes,
and Stuff You Know You Shouldn't Buy But Will Anyway.
Hang a left at the corner—stroll past Alcoholic Paradise, then
Frozen Shit You Can Leave Out for Two Weeks Without Anything
Growing On It. Scoot by Bunk Cold Remedies and
Cough Drops That Don't Work, wave
at the Exploited Child Laborers, go past the Losing Lottery Tickets
machine, out the doors, and into your vehicle.
Now drive away, unless
the Truth has already killed you.

Sin Tax

Tax the addicts. It's not like
they can quit. Build roads with the money. Improve schools.
Lower property taxes. Owning a house is
voluntary anyway. Tax the addicts
'cause they won't do what's good for them.
Make smokes 7 bucks a pack. Add cocaine
to Marlboro Lights, then tax 'em some more.
Now tax the drinkers. They're all goners
anyway. Tax the gambling addicts. Raise the cost
and lower the prize on lottery tickets.
Put a token 1-800 number on the ticket.
Don't tell people "Play responsibly." Try
"This is fun!" Now tax fast-food eaters.
They're killing themselves. Tax sex addicts.
Make 'em carry a license and registration.
Tax extreme sports participants. They're only
in it for the rush. Tax people who read
for pleasure. As if they can quit.
Now tax people who enjoy life. There oughta
be a price for that. Now tax people
who don't. For they too are guilty.

Confessions of a Flaming Liberal

I admit it. I like football.
I like football a lot. If I had to choose
between the end of football and
wearing a colostomy bag forever, well…
let's just say it would be a tough choice.
Oh, that's the least of my sins. I also
want my wife to stay home to raise
the kids. I work a lot and expect
a beer and a breather at the end of the day.
You think that's it? Nope. I can't fix stuff
but I have daydreams about it. Home improvement
fantasies, the secret wish that holding a wrench
would feel as familiar as holding…well,
other things I'm intimately familiar with.
But there are still more problems with who I am.
I don't believe in the legalization of marijuana.
Like a good boy, I do have rockstar dreams,
but play the drums barely adequately.
You want to hear more? I wouldn't rule out
voting Republican. If I had to subject
the last cow on Earth to prolonged torture
just to get the last steak on the planet,
I would. Don't get me wrong.
I believe in equal rights for homosexuals.
But I sure do like to make fun of gay people.

In Our Crappy, Crappy Economy, Here Are Some People Who've Got It Worse Than You

People who type stuff on typewriters for a living
Actors specializing in bit parts in music videos
Tap Water Celebrity Spokespeople
Honest Journalists
Diaper Service Workers
The Milkman
The Butter man
The Bread man
Men Who Make Lunchboxes Out of Metal
Men Without Hats
The Executor of the Estate of Captain Kangaroo
The Guy who came up with Pepsi Clear
The Inventor of the Salmonella Omelet
Serial Killers Who Can't Afford Things Like Night Vision Goggles
And Anthrax Spores and Whose Hands Are Too Arthritic to Cut Up
Ransom Notes Made up of Individual Cutout Letters to Send to
Maverick Detectives on the Force
Rotary Phone Repairmen
Bat Crap Farmers
Euthanasia Proponents Who Market Their Services Exclusively
To People Under Age 25
All Those Prehistoric Nostalgics Who Write Letters to the Editor
About the Good Old Days When We Were on the Barter System
And You Could Trade Two Chickens and a Handful of Beans
For a Chevy Impala
Baby Boomers, Who Are All Closing in on Death
Much Sooner Than They Care to Admit
Any Male Who Is Still Getting the Random, Prolonged,
Painful Erections of His Junior High Days Past the Age
Of 37

When Obama Was Inaugurated

for James

A light came down from the heavens
and a Voice from the sky said,
This is your President! In Him I am well pleased.

A star shone in the East
and 3 wise men traveled from afar,
laying at the feet of the newborn leader
gold, frankincense, and 787 billion dollars
in unbacked U.S. currency

Lions lay down with lambs,
a minister who hates gays prayed with one who doesn't,
Keith Olbermann and Glenn Beck French-kissed

The people who organized Hands Across America wept,
for they had finally been upstaged

Evangelical Christians felt cheated,
for the Rapture had been cancelled

and 1000 years of peace would reign
with a chicken in every pot
and a tofu chicken in every militant vegan pot
and a late-term aborted human fetus in the pots of
People for the Rights of Chickens

With a hybrid in every garage
and with all wars ended
and Palestinians singing Kum-Bah-Yah with Jews
and jihadists blessing America

and all our troubles gone up in smoke like a supervillain's last exit,
where politicians became honest,
conservatives gave a crap about their fellow human beings*
and every dirty liberal got off his welfare-cheatin' ass
and got a job.

———————————

* not just the aborted ones

26

American Teen

A few years ago
after an administrator sold it to the school board
a film crew came
to our town, our high school
to shoot a documentary

To accentuate the positive,
the administrator assured
and to show all the good things happening
at Warsaw High

So the filmmakers and crew
follow around a bunch of kids
with cameras
and reshoot scenes when
it didn't turn out
the way they wanted it to
the first time

They settle on 5 kids
who they typecast into
what the reviews call "high school archetypes"
to avoid the need
to explore who they are
as real people

And they manufacture a romance between
the hott guy and the alternachick
because every girl wants a hott guy
and girls look sexy holding guitars

And they show the rich princess
in her shittiest moments
sinking to new moral lows
because everyone knows rich princesses
are total bitches

And the geek
has to be pathetic
and crazy-acne-stained, of course

He'll be typecast for life now
or at least until his face clears up

And through editing the footage
they make it appear that the hoops star
who must be selfish, because jocks are pricks
hits a gamewinning shot

Even though he never hit
a gamewinning shot
all year

And special care is taken
to make the parents look like jackasses,
because parents of teenagers *are*
all jackasses, as every moviegoing
teenager knows

And they create ill will with the student body
by shushing the extras when shooting the stars
or by running into people while walking backwards
holding a camera or a boom mic

And near the end of the year kids
chalk onto the sidewalk
down the hall from my classroom
"American Teen Go Home"

I let them shoot
in my classroom, one period
it turned a bunch of discreetly mischievous kids
into overt seekers of their 15 minutes
and it didn't help that it was one of the worst lessons
I'd tried to teach in my less than two years on the job

I wrote a recommendation letter for the princess
much earlier in the schoolyear
praising her high character
and I hear she gets pretty nasty

in the movie
although they softened her a bit, I hear
by exploring a heartbreaking family tragedy

I really don't know
I haven't seen the film

I figure I've either lived it
having gone to our school as a kid
which would make it a waste of time to watch

Or I would know that's not how it is
at Warsaw High
which would only piss me off

I watched *Bukowski: Born Into This*
and *We Jam Econo: The Story of the Minutemen*
within the last week

A couple of documentaries with a lot of rough footage
the kind that doesn't require a second take
and I'd be willing to wager
if such things could be bet on
that both are better films

II. History

The 30th Anniversary Warsaw Community Commemorative Book Burning

scheduled for a date to be determined, winter 2007,
celebrates the 1977 reduction to ashes of "values clarification"
texts pulled off the shelves of the local high school over six months previous
to the bonfire. People Who Care, the puppet organization of a
local school board member, opposed a chapter in the book
that students, who only had access to the books under teacher supervision,
were not allowed to read. The chapter dealt with masturbation,
seen by the group as the Satanic alternative to contracting good old-fashioned
heaven-sent venereal disease. The group also burned other books found at
the high school, including *Go Ask Alice*, a nonfictional narrative
that told the story of a young woman who royally screwed up her life with drugs.
The group found the drug references objectionable.
Additionally, other "values clarification" chapters stressing the importance
of church and family were seen as opportunistic attempts to twist
the Word of God, kind of like the Satanic Bible. The 3-day gala event
will celebrate censorship and witch hunts of all kinds! Organizers
plan to drown a Wiccan, and also to symbolically censor
noteworthy historical events, including a screening of the Beatles press conference
where John Lennon proclaimed the group "bigger than Jesus"
and a subsequent burning of the projector and screen, and a loudspeaker-
broadcast of President Carter's speech declaring America to be under a
"moral malaise" and the subsequent torching of all implicated audio equipment,
as well as the grand finale, which needs your support: the destruction of any
and all history textbooks in the tri-county area that fail to
reference America as "a Christian nation" at least once. Excepting
the Wiccan, organizers claim it is a family event and no
liberals, feminists, sodomites, PETA officials, or vegans will be
officially burned in effigy. Any un-American propaganda
that surfaces at the Center Lake Pavilion, the site of the thirty-year-old deed,
shall be added to the smoldering pile of rubble, including, I have been
assured by people who care, this poem.

Dine-n-Dash with Abraham Lincoln

Dude, check it. My Dad
built a time warp to 1865 and brought back
Abe Lincoln right before he
got shot. Just walked into the playhouse
in his way nuts 21st century lab coat and coaxed him out
with, I don't know, a piece of beef jerky
or a commemorative pen or something.
Dad brought him back but didn't have time for him,
he got all wrapped up in building this pair of wax wings
he insisted I try flying high over Center Lake,
he had this evil glint in his eye, so I was like
Whoa, Dad, no, like—*no!*
so he goes, okay, then take Abe out, show him
a good time, I'm busy, and shit. He gave me fifty bucks—*score!*
so we went to Applebee's, yeah, top of the line—
Abe orders their most expensive steak
and he's like "watch me emancipate this loin
through the underground railroad of my lower intestine"
he called the steak a *loin*, it was classic.
So Abe keeps chugging Sam Adams lagers
(he reads the label aloud, "brewer patriot, aaargh!"—
he sounded like a pirate)—all I had was a Coke
and some of Abe's spinach-artichoke dip and chips,
but pretty soon I'm pretty sure we don't have the bones
to cover the tab, dig? "Ease up, Abe," I said.
"Or we'll be doin' dishes in the kitchen."
and he goes, "Do I appear to be a scullery maid?"
and I go "huh?" and he goes, "I'm not your lusty wench,
you logsplitter, you…," then he kind of yawns and goes,
"The hell you say, young Billy," cause it's a phrase
he picked up off me, you know, *the hell you say,*
"The hell you say," he goes, "I feel like we've been in this tavern
four score and seven years," and he knocks his glass
off the table with his big overgrown hand, stands up, stumbles,
goes, "I hold these truths to be self-evident!"
and then burps, farts and sneezes *at the same time*
and dig this, *he doesn't die—*

I felt like calling MythBusters or somethin'
…next thing you know, he grabs my Dad's keys
off the table and bolts out the door—I had to *dive in*
the passenger side window—and you know what?
I don't know how he is with a horse and carriage,
but Abraham Lincoln is a terrible car driver…but we make it back,
and after he wakes up from passing out, he goes,
"Billy, lad"—he called me lad—he goes, "take me back to the play,"
and I—What? What do you mean? What do you *mean*
I'm bullshitting? Dude, you *know* my Dad works for the government.

God of Thunder Joins Eco-Terrorists

In a virus-infected email sent to 2.5 million
Google mail users, Thor, the Norse god of thunder,
claimed membership in a group of eco-terrorists
known as The Green Revolution. The terrorists,
based in the Pacific Northwest with operational cells
in California, New Mexico, and Boston, are best known
for torching houses in upscale neighborhoods
and car-bombing Hummers. In the rambling,
six-thousand word document, Thor referenced
secret feelings of inadequacy when comparing himself
to his trickster brother Loki, "who's got all
the street cred, let's face it" and also noted that
a pairing of the god of thunder with the
infamous arsonist group "just felt natural."
"I can strike whole neighborhoods of yuppie Republicans
with lightning storms, and knock overconsumptive
assholes in the head with my hammer," he wrote.
Thor hinted at the possibility of an eco-strike
on fast food beef-processing plants, but hedged—
"it seems like something Hercules would do,
but I think I'm up for it." He expressed warmth toward
his eco-terrorist friends, calling them "the only humans
offering me tribute in this myth-forsaken era
of Jesus, Allah, and hedonism," and wrote that
he expected to see Norse temples built "once America
feels my wrath." He wouldn't rule out making Thursday
part of a permanent 4-day weekend "once I gain
status as the Supreme Ruler of the Universe, and stuff."

When I Peed Myself at the Bob Dylan Show

truthfully it was the Willie Nelson show
Willie Nelson's Picnic July 4 2009 Covaleski Stadium South Bend
but think about it
if Willie and Bob and John Mellencamp are playing together
even in Indiana, where Mellencamp
is the fetishized demigod of Hoosier hick rock
you're going to say you went to
the Bob Dylan show
even if he does croak through all his songs
and his delivery is oddly quick and stilted
so that a line like "Even the President of the United States
sometimes must have to stand naked"
which is supposed to elicit a rebel roar of approval
comes out sounding like
"ribbit ribbit ribbit ribbit moo?"
what I'm saying is
Bob Dylan has turned into a cowfrog
a thousand Victoria's Secret princesses can kiss him 'til their tongues blister
and he'll never sound any better anymore

so at the Bob Dylan show
we're tailgating out the back of our
$20 parking space, about ready to get in the half-mile line
and Nate goes "we could open one more beer
to stand in line with"
and I go "I already have to pee"
and Nate goes "I'm gonna sit in the car and pee
in that Powerade bottle"
it sounded good to me
exactly as adventurous as a 33-year-old dad
at a rockshow with his daughter and his buddy
and his buddy's stepson
who only planned on doing the legal drugs all night
wanted to get.
So Parker sits in there, empties into the bottle,
then Nate does, and pops out the door saying, "I filled it up,"
and I'd already cracked the Heinie and started drinking
I was committed now

He gave me a 20-ounce Culligan water bottle
with an open mouth smaller than a quarter
I got in the passenger seat, put my fleece on my lap,
couldn't jam it in there noway nohow,
my manhood's not particularly impressive,
but Parker's 8-year-old package should've been in that water bottle,
not mine,
so I figured if I just shoved it against the opening
and sealed off my dickhole
I'd be alright—but truthfully,
I had the idea I was making a horrible mistake
but I was no longer possessed of the inhibitions to stop it

I probably got a good 4 ounces in there
although I was tense, and that made it kind of hurt
then things got slippery like all half-crocked plans do
my fleece barely soaked up anything, I missed it mostly
as I squeezed and squeezed to stop the flow a puddle formed
atop my stain-resistant khaki crotch
some got on the probably fake leather seats too
I opened my door and yelled at my daughter to ask my buddy
for napkins, I don't know why she had to be the go between,
I guess we turn to family in times of crisis
when I got out I tried to cover the crotch stain with the fleece
and finished my beer with what must've been a hangdog expression
cuz Nate said, "Don't worry about it, I do it all the time"
which is the stupidest and most empathetic lie he's ever told
my daughter was less embarrassed than I expected
probably in denial
it was probably the first time she ever really wondered if she was adopted
but Parker kept flashing devil grins and shiteating glimpses
and Nate looked at him and said once "Don't"
which we all knew meant
boy, I have never done this
but I am capable of beating you like only a stepfather knows how

By the end of Mellencamp's opening set I was dried up
well enough to appreciate the historical importance
of listening to Dylan croak his way through
"Rainy Day Women #12 & 35"
in person, at least one last time before he dies.

Revisionist Literary History: Saint Hank

Saint Charles Bukowski (1920—1994),
known for feeding homeless children
with miraculously multiplying near beers
and pancake batter, wrote what are commonly
referred to as The Tomes, 78 volumes
of pristine prose and verse venerating
the horse track, the prostitute, the barfly,
the writer himself, and most importantly,
drink. 120 years after His death,
a critic dared to suggest much of His work
was mediocre, self-promoting, and overpublished,
and was burned at the stake as a heretic.
Interested Pilgrims often travel to the Shrine
of Saint "Hank," a towering cement beer bottle
on a hill overlooking Skid Row Los Angeles
that followers claim is taller than the Washington Monument.
Indeed, many theoliterary critics suggest
Saint Hank's face should grace the proverbial Rushmore
of Literary Saints, along with Pound,
Céline, and, of course, Sylvia the Courageous.

Revisionist Literary History: Medieval Women

Nobody knows about
the bra burning of 1263
where a group of serf women
invented the uplifting apparatus,
then started a bonfire in the
William the Conquerer Victory Memorial
Town Square, blazed those B-cups hot,
then hung the King's dingaling
in effigy and threw bloody
menstrual rags at passersby
shouting loudly angry slogans
like "Equal Gruel for Equal Groveling!"
and "Birthing Leave for Fieldhands!"
and "Keep Your Junk Out of My Box!"
Of course the local vassal sent knights
to halt the nonsense, but Monty Python
called it right—no matter
how many heads were decapitated or lances
run through abdomens, all the strong women
only shouted louder, like an empowerment mantra,
"Now you see the violence inherent in the system!
Now you see the violence inherent in the system!"

Top Secret Ingredients in the Coca-Cola Formula

unblessed Holy Water
rainforest bark
kidneys meant for dialysis patients
rats and snails and puppy dog tails
babies
mind control microchips
invisible robots
inactive anthrax
cloned veal
mercury found in old car hoodlights
the anger of 4 million overseas slave laborers
kilowatts
sperm bank rejects
throat cultures
petrified stool samples
hippy beard hair
cats' claws
witches' tits
essence of misunderstood genius
eau de sweaty French guy
fractions of deoxyribonucleic LSD
those 14 hours straight you spent with your mother-in-law that you'll never get back
energy stains of the undead
energy stains of restless ghosts
overpass drippings
unpasteurized ennui
evil nemesis proclamations
blood samples from bleeding heart liberals
bicycle chain grease
bionic man mojo
bisexual goo.

The End of the World

It will happen like this:
a flash on the coasts, dulled here
tripping over mountain ranges
and miles of plains.
V's of geese hitting the ground
like volleys of arrows. Electricity
blinking out in the slumbering dusk.
As usual, here in Indiana,
we won't catch on to this new trend
until it's been all up and down
the East and West coasts
timelessly marching into eternity

Things to Do in Kosciusko County When You're Sixteen Minutes from the Apocalypse

Stop, drop, and roll, and when you're sure
you still can't avoid the fire, have a drink.
A stiff one. There's liquor in the cabinet.
Unplug the phone. Your connections
will soon be less than an illusion. Pee now,
when it won't be troublesome.
Stand at the window. Look out
over the back yard. There are black squirrels
running up and down the trees.
You need something to count, besides
the spiraling seconds. Count them.

III. Faith

I don't think you have to have a clear idea of who or what God is in order to pray. You could even be quite doubtful about the whole business
—Cormac McCarthy

There ain't no devil, there's just God when He's drunk
—Tom Waits

Good Friday

it is the cook's birthday
here at the diner
with the flystrip above the grill.

An old lady in a red coat
and big glasses comes in.

She hugs him lightly, says,
"Happy Birthday, Tommy.
Jesus is dead."

How to Avoid the Angry Eyes of God

Don't cower. It's a dead giveaway.
But neither should you strut. Come out
only at night, for He is Light.
Practice blending into crowds, go places
where you may disappear amidst
thousands. I don't care what
you've heard, the Oversoul is stretched thin
when it must cover many. Despite this,
avoid home Notre Dame football games.
Drink in moderation—too much leads
to revelation, often horrible, and too little
denies you the right to weakness.
Should God tail you in an unmarked car,
drive as you normally would, do nothing
different. Go where you may without hesitation.
Should He ask you probing questions
at a party, smile politely and excuse yourself,
muttering something about "out of punch."
The greatest myth is that He prizes
your individuality. Don't ask Him to explain
the codes and maxims, nor the terrible
rewards. Think softly when alone,
as if in church. It is here,
with no one else to see or answer to,
He seeks to watch you, and to listen.

A Note to Dr. David Haines

                        thank you
for that moment at the Christmas mass
when the singer stopped singing to take
communion and you carried on
the Latin song, sonorous and deep-
hearted. It reminded me of Dad doing
the Ave Maria solo one morning
during the Eucharist, maybe off-key,
hesitant, strumming no heartstrings,
and then doing it again but with the fluid and
deep and serious tone he only maintained
while singing well. When you sang
it had been years since any true
spiritual experience in church
but I think that qualified. I want to thank you
because I so rarely dwell on his memory,
because if I didn't inherit the ability
to vocalize or the way he could be
so charmingly flakey when an audience
offered itself, perhaps I'd gotten something
better, something I can do in poems
but we can't do in our lives:
exercise the desire to do it
all over again, from the beginning,
in order to get it right.

Dark Heaven

In blank-slate first-grade nun-taught youth
I thought heaven was dark, for God so loved the world
He gave His only sun. Once spirited there,
no outdoor dodgeball could be played, swimming
was always Marco Polo and spiritual torches never stopped burning.
If the beauties of parochial school (such as the nun)
could light the way, surely Kingdom Come would shine
with at least a little radiance. But the dull moon paleness
of death refused me, even if it hadn't there was
the matter of the C's in religion and the damn-the-devil game
we played with Holy Rosaries round our necks.
Over the years, I sloughed off skin-thin faith
like so many dead cells. That is, until the blue note
crowd pumping like a Sacred Heart, soul coughing
and superchunk holding forth in the True Spirit.
Heaven was dark, back lighting casting forth
traveling preachers' silhouettes, guitars
shining like volcanic glass, cigarette smoke
and stale beer the stuff of my Elysian fields.
Preceded by a purgatory of impatient penitents
crowding near the stage, heaven stood outside of time and earth,
and yet left me wondering how it could linger so,
black marker Xs on the backs of my hands, pride
of the acolyte, stigmata afterthought of the fantastic ceremony,
walking home out there on the cold street,
in the cold night, the street-lit night
and like a choir of fallen angels the ringing in my ears.

Church League Softball

Oren and I love softball but we don't
believe in God, so we decided to collect
a team of atheists to join the church league.
We filed for entry, marking "other"
in the spot for affiliation. Our fake name
was The Church of the One, as in one life,
one chance, no soul, nothing to pray
to or for but today and tomorrow until we're dead.
The rumor spread that we were eastern mystics,
that our experience of Him bordered on the sexual.
Janice, our token woman, got a lot of attention
from opposing men. She'd wave her tight ass
back and forth in the batter's box, and they
served 'em up with a slight arc, aiming
for her sweet spot. We took a few games,
lost a few. She lead the team in ribbies,
and, she told me, aimed for the wise old man
with the long flowing beard on a low throne
of clouds just beyond the outfield
every time she connected.

Oren tried to sow the seeds of doubt
with first base banter, the devil.
Quoting directly from the old issue of *Time*,
the Jesus symposium. "What if his body
really was eaten by wild dogs?"
He posed the question to an ump,
who threw him out. It all came to a head
when the silver pentagram on a chain around my neck
flopped out of its place under my shirt and into
full view. The Baptist catcher got a good look,
struck me on the forehead with an open hand
shouting "Satan be gone!"
So I kicked him in the nuts. He wasn't
wearing a cup. Someone took pictures,
and the bench-clearing brawl put us out
of the league. But we'll go out fighting.
We're threatening to get the ACLU involved.

The Devil Is a Whip-smart Salesman

The devil is a whip-smart salesman.
He's got a vacuum cleaner that will
suck out your soul. He'll plunk that junk
down on your living room carpet and declare it
the greatest gift God gave to his mechanical
creation. "It's not a vacuum," he'll warn
teasingly. "It's a new natural order.
It will reorganize your chaos into another chaos
that never felt so free. It's a subversive
cleaning system that makes other systems seem
as a black and white dog's to your high-definition
fully realized supernatural wet dream.
It runs on lust and envy so power
is never a problem and always an issue."
The devil will spin slick rhythms
and pronounce fine pronunciations, enunciations,
emancipations and proclamations until
he's got you one fire-breathing whisper
from eternal damnation. He'll stoke 'er up,
entice you with a brief demonstration, then pull
on your soul like a laughing gas head rush
leaving you happy and stupid. Then comes
the contract, hot to the touch. "It'll pay
off," he says, "You bet it will. In time." There's
the dotted line. And there's the list
of glowing testimonials. So many
have seemed so satisfied, so many have signed.
Will you?

At the RCIA Meeting

A woman
6 months pregnant
sneaks out the door
of the church "gathering space"
for a quick smoke

my wife follows
lights up
says to the woman,
"If Jesus was pregnant,
would he smoke?"

"Jesus can't
get pregnant," the woman says

My wife says,
"Haven't you been
paying attention in there?
Jesus can do *anything.*"

Abortion Doctor Granted Nobel Prize for Creative Moralizing

The Nobel Prize Committee today recognizes Dr. Kent Masters
for "his undying commitment to the art of creative moralizing."
Dr. Masters, who boasts a record of 5318 abortions
spanning a 35-year-career of what he jokingly refers to as
"playing god with a little g" maintains
an unceasing commitment to justifying his role
as one of the country's preeminent baby killers.
Masters' equivocations include but are not limited to
the genetic discount, a 10% reduction in fees
for all mothers with IQs below 95, and a specialty in opening clinics
in blue-collar and inner-city neighborhoods because, he says,
"like we really need another welfare deadbeat crack-dealing AIDS-
infected pimp roaming the streets, and too many uneducated
hillbillies think a decent wage in manufacturing is their
God-given right." Masters is perhaps best known
for an April 1978 Planned Parenthood convention speech
where, as a young newcomer to state-certified murder,
he famously challenged Jesus to strike him with lightning
if abortion was such a bad idea, and then claimed he could whoop
10 Catholic priests at once with his scalpel hand tied behind his back,
all to thunderous applause. Dr. Masters built a thriving practice
from its humble back-alley beginnings to cover 3 midwestern states,
all of which granted him medical licenses.
He says he plans to spend the prize money "on continued
research into population control" and plans to retire
but keep busy providing abortion services part time as volunteer work,
"because you can't hold dominion over human life from a driving range."

Icons of Long-Gone Heroes Appearing Miraculously

Icons of long-respected once-forgotten saints
of the television screen are appearing miraculously
in locations across the country. The visage of Fred Rogers
was baked into a sausage pizza at a Chuck E. Cheese in Illinois,
and while the birthday girl went hungry that day, the pie did fetch
a year's tuition at a private University on Ebay. Throngs
of the faithful have since depleted the ball pit (looking for relics)
and the Pac Man joystick is said to possess powers of healing.
At the St. Louis Zoo the unmistakable form
of Captain Kangaroo graced the hide of a baby marsupial
newborn in captivity. The zoo quickly printed T-shirts,
mugs, and bumper stickers ("I brake for Kangaroo, the Holy Host")
and officials are thinking of adding a world-class aquarium
with all the extra money. The most striking development in the string
of incontrovertible evidence for an afterlife where kids' show hosts
walk hand-in-hand through fields of poppies with the Holy Ghost
is the ashen face of Happy the Hobo, seared into a Fort Wayne billboard
struck by lightning. Happy, the affable host of channel 55's
Happy's Place who always wore a painted-on shadow of a beard
was played by former youth minister Tim Jones, who, beset
by a series of providing-spiked-Kool-Aid-to-minors scandals and a hush-hush fiasco
over the impregnation of a 15-year-old virgin, committed suicide
by overdosing on Prozac in 1993. Happy's mother
says she feels it is a sign that Timmy is flying
with the angels now—in fact, you can read all about it
in her upcoming tell-all mother-of-the-icon
autobiography.

On the Day Before My Eldest Child's First Communion

If your mom and I hadn't slipped uneasily together
on a dirty couch in crazy grandma's basement
when I was getting old enough for youthful indiscretion
to mature into definitely-should-have-known-better,
I'd be doing I-don't-want-to-think-what now.
Probably not teaching. Probably still delivering pizza. Probably
thinking of her as the tragic could-have-been
of another universe, a parallel one I couldn't begin to dream.
Even though I don't believe in meant-to-be,
I know you were. That's why she thinks
I favor you, why you can melt my temper
like ice on August first. My sweet girl,
perhaps the only savior in whom
I'll ever truly have the courage to believe.

During Advent, at Mass

in one reading
God says something
unto David

5-year-old Frannie
pulls on my sleeve
"Dad! I know David!
He's a boy in my class!"

IV. Sexuality

Man delights not me—no, nor woman neither, though
by your smiling you seem to say so

—Hamlet

Royal Rumble: Gay Pride Parade and Klan Demonstration

Because the city budget was running on a deficit
and they wanted to sell the surveillance footage to
an extreme television show, and because they detest
both groups with equal fervor, Warsaw city officials
decided to schedule the Klan demonstration at the courthouse
and the Gay Pride parade around the courthouse square
one after another. The Klan had the usual smattering
of raucous inbred supporters and irate vocal opponents,
from eleven to noon spewing vitriol through megaphones
on the courthouse steps. But the hoedown really started
with the 12:05 marching of the rainbow warriors
around the town square. Three flamboyant
leather-clad dog-collared thick-mustachioed studs
pranced around the street like they were starring
in a homosexual remake of *West Side Story.* At the second
right turn around the courthouse they met with seven
white-robed gap-toothed skinhead Klansmen
sporting shit-kickers under their robes and the rumble began.
While there were more Klansmen in the melee, the gay dudes
had strong white teeth they could bite with, plus even as
the skinhead force joined their Klan brothers in whiteness
they didn't count on all the head-thumping butch lesbians
getting into the mix. They were about to end the battle with
an even draw, bruises on both sides, six compatriots down
apiece, but then a Klan member opened a cut under a
homosexual eye and got spooked at the site of blood.
"AIDS is not God's irrevocable judgment against me!"
the Klansmen gasped and his white-robed comrades
tore down their unburnt crosses, tossed megaphones into
the backs of trucks and sputtered off into the backwoods
of the countryside, while all the gay men and all the gay women
shouted out a great huzzah! and felt each other up with glee.

Homosexual Mercenaries Take Over Baghdad

"For some reason, the military seems more afraid of gay people than they are...
terrorists...if the terrorists ever got ahold of this information, they'd get a
platoon of lesbians to chase us out of Baghdad."

—*U.S. Representative Gary Ackerman, D-NY*

Actually, it took 2 flaming divisions
of gay, lesbian, bi, and transgendered Rainbow Soldiers
of the Antichrist to make our boys turn tail
and run. The GLBT Al Qaeda Alliance, they called it.
The U.S. Military, planning a counterattack, has since
issued a deck of playing cards with full-color photos
of key players from the group code-named Homo Insurgency.
You should see the ace of spades, this enormous black dude
with a 14-inch schlong who took enough hormone therapy
to grow his own set of weapons-grade knockers.
The big gay offensive mostly consisted of a barrage
of bodily fluids in latex bombs marked INFECTED shot out of
handheld rocket lauchers at our tanks, convoys, and helicopters.
The U.S. troops were grossed-out combat style and, fearing infection,
they beat a hasty retreat into the surrounding countryside.
Whodathunkit, what with Abu Graib and all. Thankfully, upon victory,
the homosexual mercenaries recruited by Al Qaeda on the empty
promise of a charter for a chain of Baghdad sex toy stores
and all the pre-teen sex slaves they could handle
turned their weapons on Bin Laden's flunkies
who beat it into the desert and the waiting weapons
of the angry and embarrassed United States troops.
The once-heavily-secured Green Zone has transformed
into some kind of fabulous disco inferno straight outta the '70s,
and the Iraqi Parliament reportedly took to the streets
dancing victory with edible panties on their heads.
Pentagon officials are in hot debate, with General Peter Pace
suggesting we could turn Baghdad into a 21st Century
Gay kind of Israel, a nation-state where we send homosexual refugees
of the U.S. culture wars and ride our missionary position homeland
out of this big, gay problem that has plagued our free and decent country,
for good.

How to Turn Yourself Into a Stalker

Hide the torrid origins
of toddler years frothing
at the mouth. Convince your parents
you're happier with no siblings.
Go to the first day of school
with dirt and drool. Read
the Encyclopedia through K.
Formulate a plan to build a porn machine
at the precocious age of nine.
Let your imagination grow longer
than your ability to converse without quaking.
Love an impossibly popular girl
from afar. Get put down
by an impossibly popular boy.
Get caught masturbating
in study hall. Crave
the attention you fear.
Develop a brain that fires
ten million times a second.
Get a financial aid package. Denounce
your home town. Estrange
your parents. Avoid
psychiatrists. See her
on a bus heading in
to campus. Begin.

Professional Advice

I went into Drugs-R(x)-Us
looking for something for my wife's nausea, not to mention
the barfing and crapping she'd been doing
all night. This kid pharmacist with a face so fresh
you could cover it in vinaigrette and eat it like a salad
came charging out from behind his counter offering help.
"My wife's got the flu," I said. "Got anything
for nausea?" "We have *this*," he lead the way,
finger crooked back at me like Captain Hook,
"but it doesn't work." "Huh?"

"What you really want to do is make her feel comfortable," he said.
"Pillows, a fan, dim the lights, keep the noise down…"
It sounded like our twice monthly ritual when the kids
miraculously fell asleep early. "What's really been shown
to help" he continued "is *touch*."

"She's been wrapped around the toilet bowl all night
head to rear and you want me to—*touch*—her?" He nodded.
"It has a proven therapeutic effect." "Alright then," I said.

I went home, checked the empty plastic bowl at her side,
blew an electric fan into her fitful sleep,
closed the blinds, knelt down next to the couch
she was hanging onto like a terminally ill panther
draped on a tree branch, and rubbed
one hand on her thigh and another on the forearm.

"What the fuck?" she started. "Get off me!
I'm half dead, you freaking necrophiliac!"
"But the pharmacist…," I said. "…the pharmacist said…"

"Where's my medicine?" she moaned, and I decided
to go back to Drugs-R(x)-Us sometime
when I was good-n-drunk, and piss on his degree.

Excerpts from My New Patient History at Northern Indiana Urology

Name: Steve Henn   **Age:** 33   **Today's Date:** 8-3-09

Referring Doctor: Dr. Pitts   **Family Doctor:** Dr. Pitts

What problem or symptoms bring you here?
I don't want to father any more children.

How severe are your symptoms?
(rank from 0 = no symptoms to 10 = very severe symptoms)
I currently have 4 symptoms. I don't believe in ranking them. I try to love them all equally.

What is the duration of your symptoms?
8 years, 5 years, 4 years, and 5 months.

Does anything make your symptoms better or worse?
(if yes, please describe)
candy = better, bedtime = worse.

Wanted: Mistress

must not ever have
to go to the bathroom.
Wineglass breasts. Clear skin.
Will drink just enough
to be willing to do anything,
within reason. Nothing
too kinky. No weird
fetishes. Nothing with feet.
Able to talk football
like a man. Must
be willing to remind
my wife, this was all
her idea in the first place.

How I Met My Wife: The Movie Version

I'm played by River Phoenix and she by,
I don't know…Sara Gilbert. The girl
who played Darlene on *Roseanne*.
We're prisoners in identically foreboding
psychiatric hospitals with a barbed-wire-strung
no-man's-land between them.
Open with a flash of lightning on a windswept night.
We've been writing letters back and forth;
although we're heavily censored, we know that s/he's
the One. When we curl our meds under our tongues
and then start to get wild, we can feel it surging
in our genitals. We have our own language now,
perfectly decipherable. A psychic spark is evident,
ecstatic flashes of a life free from the horror.
Behind barred windows, separate and together,
we are shedding neuroses, replacing dead genetics
with new sinews in our brains. Me, shaking the hand
of the doctor I couldn't bear to touch; she, making eye contact
and discussing Goya with her art therapist. At no point
does the tragic occur. We slip away on rare privileges
and consummate the relationship. There's no cheap denouement.
Nothing is final. We don't pretend like we can really know what's coming.

My Cousin Who Did a Line of Coke Off Paris Hilton's Ass

in New Orleans pre-Katrina also says
he smoked opium with Tom Delay on the catwalks
of congressional halls, says he ate mushrooms
in New Mexico with Russell Crowe, Winona Ryder and Axl Rose,
also says he watched Larry the Cable Guy saw off half
a light bulb and get geeked on crank, watched him shed 20 pounds
in 3 days before his very eyes.
But cousin Jimmy doesn't only get high with celebrities.
He had a real deep spiritual experience
with Billy Graham at a Rainbow Gathering
they held hands and jumped over a broomstick
and now they're platonically unified just like Mother Earth
and Mother Mary.
He says he fixed Jeff Foxworthy's camper engine
with nothing but a wrench and a steel guitar string
in South Dakota, at a truck stop 20 miles north of Rushmore.
Says he ran into Roger Ebert at the dollar theatre
in Fort Wayne, Indiana, and in an empty theatre Roger sat
right next to him, put his hand upon his knee.
But his epic brush with greatness is easily
running into ex-President Clinton at the Gentlemans' Club
in Kosciusko County and Bill buying him lap dances
and buying him Heinekens
and afterwards the worked-up new friends falling
into the back of a stretch limousine
getting helpful handjobs from Secret Service agents
about whom cousin Jimmy says he's been sworn to secrecy.

Minivan Warrior

I've heard guys talk
about the minivan
like it's step one down the road
to eternal impotence
but when I'm at the helm
of our family cruiser
wife riding shotgun
three kids in carseats behind us
I imagine
driving it into battle and mowing down Nazis
or driving it into the White House
and honking all the stupid
out of Bush's brain
or offroading, spraying mud up
on the flat roof 'til it drips
down the windows
or drag racing down 15
cocky teenagers spun out
in my wake
I imagine it a mystery machine
a love machine
a shag rug carpeted
cock-compensation magic machine
and then I pull into the Dollar General
down by the Big Lots
leave my wife to tend the kids
and make off with a jumbo pack of diapers
like a Viking pillaging a village

Novelty Item

I ran afoul of the law
the other day; shoplifting
a rubber chicken at the novelty store
in the mall. It reminded me
of an old girlfriend, the way it lay there
lifeless, but as if it could quiver
if it wanted to. I adjusted my pants
to hide the erection, standing there amid
strobe lights, fart sprays, silly string
and a display of thick cartoon books,
"illustrated dirty jokes." That chicken…
I picked it up and brought it to my face,
inhaling the odor, the taste.
The things that we could do,
alone, together. I had these long
tube socks on, a little loose from wear,
and I pulled up my pants leg and tried
to stuff the chicken halfway up the torso
into one sock, but a clerk approached
and I got spooked and ran, forgetting
to let go of the chicken. Mall Security
caught me in the parking lot, weeping,
banging my shins and forearms against
automobiles, declaring it all a mistake.
I got off with a warning and a banishment,
which is okay, the place has got
a crummy arcade anyway. I keep having
these dreams, though. My old girlfriend's body,
rubber chicken from the neck up.
Now I sweat walking by the eggs
in the grocery store, as if they connect
she and I like rubber stretched and busted,
the almost-weres of a sick fantasy,
the illegitimate children of my wet dreamscape.

At the Shrink's II: The Magazine Rack

I checked in at the shrink's office—
it's one of those multinational corporation shrink's offices
where they've got like 85 doctors working there and a secret plan
to install a local shadow government—and I walk by
the magazine rack full of *Ladies' Home Journal* and *ESPN* magazines—
as if some crazy person is going to pass the time reading
an article on quilting or the size of Barry Bond's head—
and there's this magazine called *Out!*—it's a magazine for
gay people—*Out!* get it, like—"yep, I'm gay"—
and it got me curious, I have to admit, not *sexually* curious,
don't get me wrong, not like I'm wondering what it's like
to have some sweet lover man's stubble rubbing against my cheek—
but just curious about what kind of stuff you put
in a magazine for gay people—but I didn't want to pick it up,
and I didn't want to stand there and stare at it and have some
sexual predator who's being sedated to control his urges size me up—
so I just caught one headline on the cover, it was something about
nude gladiator mud wrestling. I know, it sounds like
I'm trying to be a dick, but it's true—I sit down
too far away to read the cover, next to this guy in short shorts
holding an oversized teddy bear (it was weird, I kept
imagining him in diapers) and then I started giggling because
I was imagining an article on how to tell your parents you're gay,
and I thought the best way would be to get one of those planes
to trail a banner around the sky above their house, you know—
"Mom and Dad, I'm gay. Don't hate me. Love, Jeremy"—
and my doctor called me back, and I was trying to stop giggling, and
I was shaking and all that, so he increased my doses
and everything, which sucks, because it's really
slowed down my thinking, I can hardly put two sentences together, really.

The Homosexual Agenda

I met a traveler from an antique America
who said, "The gays are taking over. It is ruining
our country. Someone has got to put a stop
to the homosexual agenda." I replied:
"Yes. Someone has got to infiltrate their
lair deep in the bowels of San Francisco—
have you heard of it? It's like the frigging
Justice League, or Superman's arctic ice hideout.
Truth be told, the only reason they set up
like they're superheroes is because they think
the outfits are fabulous. Seriously, since they're
trying to recruit our kids for a Gay America
and poison our children's brains with their damn
subliminal messages about how groovy
sodomy is, somebody should gather up a bunch
of action hero movies like Sylvester Stallone
in *Rambo* or *Over the Top* or anything
with Steve McQueen or Charles Bronson
and project them onto gigantic movie screens
set up in the heart of places like Boystown
in Chicago, we could even trick 'em into
coming to see the flicks by advertising free
moustache rides and stuff, and then when
we play the action hero movies it'll be just
like kryptonite and all the gay dudes will fall down
and go, "Aaaaah! Aaaaaaah! Errrraaaaah!"
and melt like wicked witches—" and the traveler
interrupted, saying, "What about the lesbians?"
And I said, "What? What do you mean what
about the lesbians? I just figured, with all
the secret porn stashes of He-men across
the nation, that hot lesbians are perfectly acceptable.
Aren't they?"

V. *after* **Ginsberg**

(Sigh)

for Zeb Stevenson

I.

I saw the best minds of my hometown destroyed by domesticity, thirsty,
       tired, having to take a piss,
dragging themselves down the staid and sober Center Streets of
       Indiana in old cars on a 10 p.m. Thursday trying to avoid the cops,
levelheaded fathers mothers husbands wives with white hot love doused by
       children car payments income taxes parent teacher conferences
who paycheck to paycheck and credit card owing and alcohol buzzed sat
       on stools at Bennigan's Ruby Tuesday Applebee's drinking beer
       specials lamenting the state of everything
who went fishing in mercury-filled lakes stinking of summer sewage
       wondering how in this economy am I going to get a job
who passed out children with light in their eyes and swore never to raise
       them as their mothers and fathers did and then did
who dropped out of school when administrators decided that the tattooed
       the longhaired the gay the bi the 16 year old living on her own
       were part of the problem not part of the solution
who lost their sweet 16 virginity to 23 year old creeps and cried in the Dairy
       Queen walk-in freezer and thanked a God who might not be there
       for the negative pregnancy test
who got busted for bringing dogs and skateboards to a public park but
       whose McDonald's cups full of ½ Coke ½ tequila went undetected
with dreams local as corn, mature, ironic, with jobs without imagination,
       with a seat on a barstool next to an orthopedic company doctor-
       consultant shilling for Zimmer hips who never bought a round for
       anyone but himself
incomparably average and drowning in their mean median mode
       middleness wanting to be Bob Dylan or Man Ray but never
       Mellencamp, shouting distance and 35,000 lives from Chicago
slinging pot and avoiding arrest and driving carefully and then settling
       down into a real job which is a job with benefits that can be done
       forever endlessly without thinking, head in a nothing box sharing
       stories at age 27 of the carefree good old days when every girl was
       youthful and boys' backs not bowed by responsibility
who buckled themselves into Fastcabs for 10 dollars a ride plus tip when
       they'd had so much they couldn't steer straight and had the driver
       stop by Taco Bell and puked in the cab which was actually a navy
       blue minivan with a no smoking sign

who played cornhole all night in backyards and yelled at toddlers to stay
out of the way and made them cry and apologized and lifted them
onto their shoulders and even let them throw 4 in the hole and
sign the board with a scribble
who listened to Chicago Cubs on crackly radio doing dishes in the kitchen
because cable cost too much
who spent so much on beer and cigarettes they could've had cable and a
Blackberry and a BluRay player but settled for YouTube and email
and in some cases Internet porn
Fox News gawking on the bar TV and listening to local felons gripe that they
can't stand to look at the face of the new black President
whole intellects marinating in regret and Miller Lite and incubating a
minuscule seed of possibility that something's got to give our
garage band will get signed a stranger at the bar will offer a job so
cake it's like vacation our children will grow into professional
athletes
who vanished into their adoptive parents' country houses to kick oxycontin
cutting their hair from 14 inches to one half inch
reappearing in a contemporary church service on Sunday which is
a church service with electric guitars
suffering hangovers and secret swine flus caught from children in the
waiting rooms of urgent care facilities
who saw their old high school English teacher walking around downtown 2
a.m. with a cigar in his mouth and asked him What're you up to and
heard Taking a walk. How the hell're you?
who still can't shake cigarettes unless they've been pregnant or their wives/
girlfriends have and who plan to quit as soon as the next season
turns
who quote South Park Simpsons Family Guy and whose fathers run local
businesses or are retired but who know only one true father and
that is Pop Culture
who drove to Etna Green once and drank at the only bar and drove home
without dying or getting arrested
who have at least three friends who've been psychiatric inpatients and who
are outpatients themselves, or could be
who listened to a fight start in a limousine at a bachelor party in
Indianapolis but you never saw a punch thrown, who in fact have
never thrown a punch only threatened to
who never fucking went anywhere, who thought about it but what about
that one hippy called Turtle who left town and became a crack
addict and a carnie and returned but nobody wants to be seen with
him in public anywhere

who disappeared into the game preserve when 17 and dropped acid or
what they thought was acid and claimed to have seen the face
of God which was laughing but they couldn't tell—laughing at
them or with them

who burned their calves with cigarettes and tattooed themselves with
guns their mothers kept in Boggs Addition where children can't
go out in daytime for fear of pedophiles

who read poems at local open mic music nights and were usually booed
or ignored but occasionally greeted with hoots and hollers and
fuck-yeahs

who refused to break down crying when their mothers found breast
lumps but instead called a buddy and swallowed a pitcher and
told him all about it which was much cheaper than a shrink

whose only crimes were drinking crimes and who were passionate only
while drinking and who constantly tried to give up or cut down
on drinking but couldn't

who stood in their work van at their cubicle in the back room in the
bathroom in the faculty lounge in the mailroom and let out
one deep (sigh) and carried on

who boasted of sexual escapades in the most roundabout way and who
gave their number to every girl they saw and hit on strippers
and screwed 40 year old Miss Indianas but spent long months
in celibacy after months of false starts and disappointing sex

who played cornhole in the wind in March in 50 degree weather on
wet ground because it was the first time in 4 months they
could have a beer outside

who joked about having sex in public places but never did; who only
discussed positions on a guys-only camping trip

who lost their children to ex-wives and lost their jobs to economic
downturns and lost their unemployment checks to pitchers of
Coors Light

who decided to have a baby and made it happen on the first try or who
went off birth control for two weeks and it happened or who forgot
the spermicide on purpose because they wanted it to happen, but it
always happened, it was bound to happen, and who attributed this
to destiny and not biology

who went to karaoke nights where 50 year old horndog emcees made
dirty jokes and winked at mentally retarded women and who were
in the bar with 5000 guys and 2 single girls and 3 married
women who had left their husbands at home on purpose

who went out to the same places and drank the same drinks and did the
same things and played the same three songs at the open mic every

week because those were the songs they could trust themselves to
get right when drunk

who got so fucking tired of people playing Last Dance with Mary Jane just
because it's got a line about Indiana boys they called out the whole
scene in a poem and for a short time, nobody played it, praise Jesus

who swore to God about the greatness of action movies and special effects
and who snuck candy into the local theater so their kids could eat
M&Ms and watch Pixar animation

who jumped out of their brother's moving car at a stoplight when he was
driving drunk and crazy in January and walked to a friend's house
and didn't want to wake his kids so slept in his delivery van in
15 degree cold

who thought about suicide for a nanosecond but knew enough people who
actually tried that they didn't take themselves too seriously and
went out and bought a case instead

who never ate hot wings, no matter how low the price

who wept only for the births of their children

who at 17 sat on streetcorners playing guitar and bongos like the damned
beatniks they thought they were when a woman came out of a
house across the street and yelled We're trying to sleep!

who worked in buildings without elevators because no building is taller
than the courthouse and who in the courthouse only took the stairs

who brought their notebooks to the bars but instead talked through
diversions of football and wives and husbands and lovers you want
but can't have all to avoid whatever dull and macabre epiphany
writing would lead to

who grilled deer burgers given to them by a guy at work sizzling hot in
order to kill the worms he said might be in there

who were plunged into kiddie pools by their husbands or wives and soaked
their socks and cell phones and screamed god damn it

who said god damn it and fuck you and bullshit in front of their kids all the
time, and who were raised in the vicinity of gangsta rap, but who
never said the c-word in front of a female, not even in a poem

who stopped wearing a watch the second year that they started carrying
around a cell phone all the time

who went to high school in the years of dial-up when no one had a cell
phone and no one's parents ever really knew where they were when
they weren't home

who while that happened might've been parked behind the middle school
with their finger in a 15 year old freshman girl or tongue on a
17 year old dropout boy or drinking at the game preserve or taking
long drives in the country to smoke

who jumped off a grain silo and broke their legs which doctors filled
    with pins forever and who couldn't run anymore and got into
    the Grateful Dead because they felt bad about themselves

who thought Kurt Cobain was God when they were 16 but twice
    the life later realized what a douche he was to kill himself and
    never listened to Nirvana anymore anyway because that was
    then

who rode shotgun to Stimmelator's strip club less drunk than the
    driver and drank Rolling Rock and got boobs of sickening sweet
    perfume in their mouth and never got off and came home to
    same sex roommates

who hitchhiked to Claypool, who sat in a treehouse in Claypool playing
    flashlight chicken training a video camera on cops, who 17 yrs
    old sat on the picnic table next to the only bar in Claypool and
    watched a drunk county cop stumble out and shoot a hole in
    the stop sign

who rediscovered Independence fireworks at Winona Lake Park when
    their kids were old enough to oooh and aaaah and who 30 yrs
    old wanted to tear their hair at the ecstatic exclamations of
    latter day hippies who are nothing more than teenagers who'll
    do sexual favors for hallucinogenics

who did 15 weeks in the county jail for possession and who never
    touched a joint after that because the pot around here wasn't
    that good and jail wasn't worth it

who calculated lottery winnings from the Bennigan's barstool and built
    hotel-bar-coffeehouses in their heads and for whom retirement
    was an equally enticing myth

who were prescribed antidepressants and antianxiety and ADHD drugs
    and who used and abused and disabused themselves of them
    who swore never to take them again before scheduling
    appointments to get more

who swore never to return to Catholic church or any church once 18
    but who saw their kids baptized in the same church where they
    were confirmed

who if they hated Christians didn't hate friends who were Christian and
    if they were Christian didn't condescend to proselytize to
    non-Christian friends

who were terrified and comforted by and ambivalent about and
    counting on keeping the same job for the next 40 years even
    though out beyond in the world that turns no one kept the
    same job for 40 years anymore anywhere

returning 8 years past graduation to teach at the school they graduated

to work at the businesses their fathers owned to worship in their
    mothers' churches
with Mark Judy Frances Nancy Anne Mike Dan—parents wise too late for
    their wisdom to be valued who back-when friends tried to shock but
    couldn't who held their hands as they rockingchaired in chronic
    illness or cancer and whisperhissed you're right, you're right,
    you've always been right
ah, Zeb, while you remember Bloomington I remember Bloomington, and
    Alaska, and Jefferson School playground, and that house in Winona
    Lake, like a numb twitch on an eyelid on an eyeball looking
    backward
and who therefore thirst to bless what they cursed to affirm cornfields and
    county roads to affirm flat land and stinking lakes to affirm
    churches on every corner and bars in between to deny they ever
    denied like Saint Peter and Pope Benedict and Roger Clemens
who dreamt a life beyond the city county state limits and never made it,
    who dreamt a life free from family and fathered and mothered
    children, who dreamt pot induced and acid soaked consciousnesses
    but were smart enough to deny these for the lesser evil of alcohol,
    or in your case, Zeb, for 9 years without either smoking or
    getting drunk
to recreate the lives their parents lead only with different jobs or different
    faiths or the same faiths or different genders of children, to discard
    ideology like a negative pregnancy test but to embrace tradition
    even if they never had it, to care for their children even if they
    weren't cared for themselves, to understand what their parents
    couldn't
the sanest people we know, ourselves, who spent time on psychiatric wards,
    who lay claim to our own sanity, who call the teachers and doctors
    and parents now old who called us insane insane themselves
and rise as our own mothers and fathers reincarnated and transformed
    and who write songs about our children and who still write songs
    and poems about each other
with the suffocation and freedom of loving our spouses, our children,
    loving ourselves
with the suffocation of the homes we were destined to inhabit
with the suffocation and freedom of our overtime jobs and our overtime
    parenting
with the suffocation and freedom of not having a job and wanting one
with the knowledge that we can only be free when we embrace the
    struggle,
hallelujah, amen, amen and again amen

II.

Who built this town we hate and love and hate to love and can't get away
        from and ever always return to—
Billy Sunday, damnable damner of alcohol! Billy Sunday leaking like
        inebriation into the brains of local leaders and pastors! Billy
        Sunday who is the reason I chose Catholicism!
Moral Billy Sunday whose morals precede reason! Billy Sunday
        book puncher and Bible thumper! Censor Billy Sunday, spiritual
        ancestor of the 1977 book burnings!
Billy Sunday whose polar opposite is local English teacher Jack Musgrave!
        Billy Sunday who shits on the secular! Billy Sunday for whom
        anything secular is everything profane!
Billy Sunday fundamentalist! Billy Sunday where Grace College Basketball
        Camp repeats the mantra FUNDIES ARE FUN! Billy Sunday who
        would never use the term *mantra*, who would consider *mantra*
        profane and who believed in prayer and only prayer and if a child
        needs bread give him prayer instead!
Billy Sunday for whom prayer means telling people what they're doing
        wrong! Billy Sunday who prays for the damnation of alcoholics!
        Billy Sunday who played White Baseball! Billy Sunday who saved
        his best prayers for White Baseball players!
Billy Sunday who entered my soul from the frowns of elders! Billy Sunday
        who equates sex with shame! Billy Sunday for whom girls must be
        virginal and pure and never swear!
Billy Sunday who would easily lose a cosmic fist fight with Ambrose Bierce!
        Billy Sunday who if he came back wouldn't be caught dead in Rex's
        Rendezvous where when it was called something else Ambrose
        Bierce worked! Billy Sunday whose Civil War was all about showing
        civilians the errors of their ways!
Billy Sunday who Carl Sandburg denounced for your back flips and your
        bullshit and your passing of the collection basket! Billy Sunday
        who elevated dogma and denied mysticism! Billy Sunday who loves
        when God makes rules but hates when He shows mercy! Billy
        Sunday self-proclaimed gatekeeper of salvation!
Billy Sunday who is the stink of sewage in summer in Winona Lake! Billy
        Sunday whose legacy is 4000 uptight old men shaking
        their pointy fingers at kids! Billy Sunday who wouldn't baptize
        anyone in Winona Lake for fear of a dead fish floating up their ass!
        Drowning in the lake! Covered in sewage! Floating in Cherry
        Creek where the dead trees line the shores!

III.

Zeb Stevenson! I'm with you in Atlanta
      where Warsaw, Indiana, must seem a million miles away
I'm with you in Atlanta
      where not drinking and not smoking must feel very strange
I'm with you in Atlanta
      where I envy you for being able to talk to your dad
I'm with you in Atlanta
      where I know how it must hurt to talk to your dad because of the
      shape he's in
I'm with you in Atlanta
      where we are world renowned artists and my canvas is a page
I'm with you in Atlanta
      where you don't know you made it into the Warsaw *Times Union*
      for "On this day/15 years ago"
I'm with you in Atlanta
      where I share stories of my children and my vasectomy
I'm with you in Atlanta
      where your need to take psychiatric drugs has disappeared with
      your need to take other kinds of drugs
I'm with you in Atlanta
      where you're a workaholic like I am
I'm with you in Atlanta
      where you accuse your soon to be bride of being too real and have
      a paranoid moment where she turns into your first girlfriend
      Kathleen
I'm with you in Atlanta
      where all our ex girlfriends reveal what douchebags we used to be
I'm with you in Atlanta
      where you may never share your father's faith but where surely you
      are glad he has it
I'm with you in Atlanta
      where every mad Mexican worker freaks over the kitchen prep
      when you walk down the line six foot one red all over speaking
      fluent Spanish
I'm with you in Atlanta
      where my heart aches for your childlessness simply because my
      daughter Zaya saved my soul and where yours might not need
      saving but where a child would grow it even larger

I'm with you in Atlanta
>   where your preacher father Mark mutters gibberish in pain 24
>   hours a day, where your mother Judy is a saint but not the type
>   of saint who does no wrong or never judges or always loves but the
>   kind who is genuine and capable of patience and kindness and
>   giving and receiving forgiveness

I'm with you in Atlanta
>   where your ear was on the phone when James and I said we were
>   road tripping to your wedding

I'm with you in Atlanta
>   where we'll still drive road tripping through flat plains and hillbilly
>   mountains and marshes and clay and peanut farms, maybe not this
>   summer when you're getting married, but someday damn it, when
>   we're all happy with the place we're in, when the world ceases
>   beating us down, when we stop thinking of God as another version
>   of The Man as I have stopped thinking of Him, when our
>   restlessness fades like an old libido, when you can stay and I can go
>   back to Warsaw, Indiana, without the slightest hint of regret

VI. Third Person

She stretches the truth with such imagination
She's more of a writer than a liar.

—*Daniel Johnston*

Myrtle Beach

Our 1987 family vacation was something special.
My mom, dad, bro, sis, grandma, grandpa all stacked
into the seven-seater station wagon with the fake wood design
running down its sides. Myrtle Beach sounded pretty sweet,
thanks to *Sports Illustrated* I had recently discovered
the things I could do to myself after getting an eyeful
of hot girls in bikinis. Somewhere in West Virginia
grandpa hit senility, pooping all over himself
and the seat behind mom. "Piss," my father said, then
grandpa did, and we found a rest stop ASAP.
Dad rummaged through supplies, uncovering a 15-foot hose,
of all things. "Undress!" he told the old man. It was mom's
dad, who in his better days gave my father hell for working
at a shipping hub of a trucking company, instead of, I don't know,
teaching in the Ivy League. "Here, Ryan," dad told me.
"Take this 'ere hose over to that 'ere faucet and give your granddad
a good hosing off." It seemed to me like
just the opposite of wet girls in bikinis. I sprayed grandpa
'til the water running off his ass ran clear
while dad smoked a Pall Mall unfiltered and mom wrung her hands
and contorted her face with worry. When
we got to Myrtle Beach I had myself a rather
frustrating puppy love fling with a 13 year old named Samantha
which resulted in my first, second and third wet dreams,
but she remains no more than a hazy memory.
Grandpa's shitty ass will be stuck to the backs
of my eyelids for as long as I can see.
I couldn't stop thinking of it at his funeral,
shed tears like a clogged gutter
on a rainy day when we flung Holy Water
on the casket and they lowered it
into the ground as the sprinkler system
turned on at the cemetery.

Gil's 10,000th Beer

A Cal Ripken of drinking, Gil
spent 1667 consecutive days
downing six-packs of anything
American—Coors, Budweiser,
Sam Adams, Miller, various and
sundry microbrews—after year one
he ate only one protein-heavy meal
a day and took a multivitamin,
wanting to stay in playing shape.
He didn't have alcoholism
in his genes but persevered,
and so the streak became
a testament to his own cirrhotic
willpower. It was easy
to work-in his brother's wedding,
coworker's promotions, the night out
buying his brother beers to celebrate
his firstborn, but harder to manage
Easter and his mother's birthday
and those Indiana Sundays
he'd have to plan ahead for.
He even had to go begging for supplies
from a reliably alkie friend
when his ATM account ran dry
one Sabbath and he only had 3 Rolling
Rocks from an eighteen-pack
left in the fridge.
On that luminary and culminating day
when his fourth brew marked the apex
of his achievement, he was alone,
as he had planned it. This was his
victory, his ceremony, his rite
of passage. He thought about calling
the Guinness Book people—fittingly—
but decided someone in Ireland
had probably outdone him. It was
the 4th of July. He sat half naked on a folding
lawn chair on the awningless slab of concrete

that posed as a back porch
and watched the fireworks go off
over the fairgrounds in the distance,
each burst of light a celebration
of what had long since ceased to shine
inside him

Identity Theft

We live on the edge of two neighborhoods.
The neighborhood next to us is considerably more
affluent, so naturally, I snuck over to the neighbor's house
at 3 a.m. on a Monday morning and began digging
through their trash. I applied for two credit cards in the husband's
name. He had a credit line of 50 grand, twice over,
which worked out well for me. We ate out a lot, bought rounds
of drinks for the bar, got clothes, spent thousands of dollars
on chairs that massaged as you sat in them, but I grew bored,
and then bought a telescopic camera lens for my $2000 camera
and started taking pictures. Noticed the way the neighbor
parted his hair and flossed his teeth, got a shot of the name brands
on his Oxford shirts, his wristwatch, and bought my own.
I got a cash advance and hired a private dick
to record the weight when he steps on the scale and the position
in which he services his trophy bride. My wife
was angry when I put on fifteen pounds on purpose,
angrier still when I demanded she call me "Larry"
and asked her if, during the deed, I could call her Sue.
I bought a Lexus just like his and, having quit my job
after coming into all this money, decided to start showing up
at his office, taking on the mannerisms that the investigator assured
me were his. Larry was not an old man but became bewildered
when I took over his position as Vice President of Sales
and was locked away on a high-security psych ward
when the fraudulent bills I brought his way came through the mail.
I started going over there once again in the middle of the night
for an insomniac snack, then started staying for coffee in the morning,
then when I got home from his job began watching sports on TV there
in the late afternoon. My wife moved out of that run-down bungalow
I used to live in next door and has taken up with some beatnik drifter
hippie pot trafficker type, which is fine with me. I didn't have any kids
with her to support, but every day I play catch with Larry's boy
in the backyard, and ever since we offered to host the office Christmas party
I've got plans to make and stuff to do.

Questions from Students

Q: Mr. Henn, what were you like in high school?
A: Thinner.

Q: Mr. Henn, why did you become a teacher?
A: For the prestige.

Q: Mr. Henn, have you ever smoked pot?
A: Have you?

Q: Mr. Henn, what were you doing at the bar at Bennigan's last night?
A: Drinking.

Q: Mr. Henn, who are you voting for?
A: The lesser of two evils.

Q: Mr. Henn, do you believe in God?
A: Like a physicist believes in String Theory.

Q: So, Mr. Henn, you mean you're like, *for* the gays!?
A: Yep.

The Great Corn Detasseling Poem

I asked our department head why
in all the English Education journals
every mention of teaching poetry to teens
specifies the setting as the Urban high school.
She quoted a retired teacher who'd say
We have yet to produce the Great
Corn Detasseling Poem. But it exists
as surely as toilet-papered front yard trees
in October; in June cornfields you can stand
and hear it growing. Its cousins
are playing chicken to see which of them
will first be plastered onto the page.
The Great Underage Drinking at the Game Preserve Poem
remains confident in its own indestructibility,
the Great Skipping Class for McDonald's Breakfast Poem
is sure it won't get caught with greasy fingers,
the Great Fistfight at Carr Lake poem is twitching
to prove itself, the Great I Raised Myself and Buried
Two Alcoholic Parents Poem is beating on the coffins
as the light goes dim, the Great If Only
My Face Would Clear Up Poem is riddling
a teenage notebook with pus, the Great
My Uncle Has a Meth Lab in his Trailer Poem
is clawing at its own skin and begging mercy
from the air, while the Great Corn Detasseling Poem,
long ago filtered into the soil, worn into thin
T-shirt sweat stains in mid summer, reaches upward,
a tendril promising nourishment
for all the unbelieving ears.

Poem in the Manner of a Beatnik Hipster Psychobabbler Writing an Introductory Essay to a Newly Published Book of My Poems

This Henn cat's jive is
marmalade marijuana, exploding ecclesiastics,
dark horse apocalypse, fa la la.
Henn gets jiggy like a thin lizzy frigging,
playing this little piggy with the wigglies
of the overlord foes, can you dig it?
Hootenanny psychopath, that's what I'm
talkin' 'bout! Fat jazz in an obese world,
dig? So I had to let the word speak.
Plus, the book was free.

Promotional Considerations

People in McDonald's commercials are never fat and always want to have
    sex with their Quarter Pounders.
Joe Camel never had to stick a microphone on his throat to talk.
People in Dorito's commercials never have orange skuzz on their fingers.
Cars in commercials never travel straight boring potholed roads lined with
    corn and speed traps.
This billboard near my house advertising hair removal doesn't show a
    before shot of the hairless lady's back.
Every woman wearing perfume advertised in print has legs to her neck and
    wears an evening gown with a slit to the hip.
Why the hell is Bob Dylan endorsing Victoria's Secret?
    And where's the shiteating grin, Bob?
    Bob? Those are underwear models. How
    am I supposed to trust you if you don't wear a shiteating grin?
Notre Dame enrollment promotions always mention tradition, never cost.
Only beautiful babies wear Pampers and Huggies.
Ugly ones have to wallow in their own filth.
Did you know its fun as all hell to blow a paycheck at a casino or on a ten-
    yard-long roll of Hoosier Lottery scratch-offs?
The ladies in the late-night loveline ads are never apparently carrying the
    herpes virus.
Ads promoting the WNDU weather team make it seem like missing the
    forecast results in a death worse than fate.

Nine Non-Lethal Uses for Your Standard Issue Suicide Machine

1. dinner party centerpiece
2. cold air vaporizer for your infant's bedroom—be sure
   to remove the cyanide droplets
3. the companion who never leaves your side,
   the syringe-studded buddy you can count on
4. emergency parachute for ground-floor apartments
5. the place where you keep dead body parts—fingernail
   collection, and eyelashes, and pubic hair, and kneecap
   scrapings
6. have it delivered to your ex on Valentine's Day,
   in lieu of the let's-get-back-together roses
7. it makes for a kickass beer bong
   (little known fact)
8. shrine to all the pointless gods
9. as a testament to your empty life: you find
   it is your only indestructible possession.

VII. First Person

I am an incurable, and nothing else behaves like me.

—*Robert Pollard*

The Deer

It may have been in the twenties,
no wind, stars out. I stood
on the front porch, aware of
but immune to temperature, inhaling
stale tobacco, thinking about
how much time I had
until the baby woke up.

A group of deer—six,
eight maybe—came loping
from the side of the house
and froze: all facing the
lit neighborhood street
solid like lawn ornaments,
like statues, obviously lost.

They didn't see me. You'd think
they'd smell the smoke, but
they never turned their heads.
I did what any right-thinking
hardily-constituted young man would:
I gave chase. They scattered;
I followed three small does across
the street and into the neighbor's back yard.

Everything went very fast and yet
I noted every changing, momentary terrain
as if I were a geologist—off the porch,
into my patchy yard, the hard black street,
the neighbor's soft grass. I must have thought
of myself as a linebacker or a Neanderthal,
though I've never played organized football
or studied anthropology.

                    The deer came to a
fence, two split each way but the middle one,
the smallest, hit the fence and I tackled it,
I brought her down hard.
I lay on it, holding it in a neck-lock

saying, "What about that, huh?!"
and then, "I own you! I *own* you!"
I expected it to say something,
to protest or curse or tell me, "look buddy,
I'm not the one who pooped in your yard."
We were both breathing hard, my chest rising
and falling, the deer on her side body rising
and falling. I softened my grip on her
and said, "You've got some pair of lungs,
don't you?" It said nothing, only gasped
and then struggled, rearing its head
and kicking its legs and I knew
it was time for us to part.

It stood unsteadily but quickly,
began to hunker off, gain its step and
gallop away, and I found myself
lying there on the cold, moist ground
exhilarated, breathless, wondering,
Is that deer beaten or proud? and,
Am I beaten or proud? The scent of her
was on me and also the scent
of grass, and I found myself
wishing that had been
the way that I'd met my wife.

I Stole This Nasty Prank and Made It into a Poem

Oren thinks it would be funny
to fill up a grocery cart at the local supermarket
with sixty bucks worth of alcohol, cigarettes,
diapers, formula, and lottery tickets. Then,
when you try to pay with a fifty
and the clerk informs you that you're short,
put back the diapers and the formula.
Do so without pause. Snicker
as you give 'em reason for their hearts to bleed.

The Egg Problem

Our next door neighbor happened over one afternoon
after my wife had gotten into the better part
of a bottle of wine. He had 66 large white eggs,
3 cartons of 18 and another dozen, and he thought
we should have them. "Oh, *thank you*," she said,
just as if she were completely sober. "Thank you *so* much.
We could really use these!" She seemed so excited
that he came back with another 12. She sobered up
before I got home. We had 78 eggs. What
could we possibly do with them all? We couldn't eat them
all, could we? For three days we tried.
Scrambled for breakfast, poached for lunch, and Eggsaronious
for dinner. The children started turning sickly shades
of yellow and white. We bickered. "Why can't you make the eggs
tonight?" "You do it, I'm tired of making the eggs!"
"I'm about to stick eggs up your goddamn ass!"
"...I'm sorry." "I love you..." but the bliss
didn't last. With 3 kids, there's no time
for make-up sex. We became agitated.
Started thinking that the eggs were in there,
in the fridge, plotting against us, planning
to come out and take over the house, rub us out,
adopt the children and ship them off to Catholic
boarding school where every day is Easter Sunday.
We finally gathered them up one Tuesday night
just as they were starting to turn bad and after the kids
were in bed, walked across the yard and lobbed
them one by one by one again, against the front
of the offending neighbor's house, our anxious nerves healing
with each shell-crack against the painted aluminum siding.

How to Succeed in Rock-n-Roll without Really Trying

To be a great drummer
I must cultivate anger,
laugh with ferocity,
make enemies in order
to hold them in contempt,
bust through heads
with sticks every rhythm-honed
practice, snarl, spit,
learn to lose the friendly drunk
demeanor or better yet
wear my sobriety
like a clenched fist—
I must hate knowing people,
scowl often, connect
to bass and rhythm guitar
as blood flows through bone,
I must be denied every other
outlet, incapable of singing,
too frustrated to write a simple line,
I must have it in for someone
every time I sit behind the kit.

Daydream

I had this daydream
while washing my hands
in a public restroom,
thinking, what if you guys died,
my wife, my daughter,
some horrific accident,
run over while pushing the stroller
down the street, lapsed
into coma, expired days later.
I took this perverse pleasure
in imagining the bender I would go on,
the glorious self-destruction,
the fuck-you to God and all the world.
I walked out of the restroom, thinking,
am I, as they say, a glutton
for punishment, a rank destructive pervert—
or not, because then I imagined
all the sober time
of you not being there, and
the grief went flush behind my eyes,
and I had to keep telling myself
it isn't true, it isn't,
because I had to go to class,
but I wanted to call you,
to make sure that you were alright.

Scenes from a Movie about My Wife and I Arguing over Having More Kids

This is the part where she tries to call and cancel my vasectomy.

This is the part where I tell her again that I've only been teaching 5 years and we have 4 kids and she stays at home.

This is the part where she tries to convince me to play Russian Roulette with my junk two days before my vasectomy and 5 months after her last labor, where she asks me to just do it and see if it's meant to happen.

This is the part where I tell her this is one thing whether meant to happen or not that I don't want happening.

This is the part where she cries in bed after she thinks I fell asleep and I lay there motionless and breathing evenly.

This is the part where she finally falls asleep and I get up and look at myself in the bathroom mirror for a really long time.

This is the part where she says What if we win the lottery? Will you reverse it? You have to.

This is the part where I imagine having ten kids and a full time nanny and never having to work.

This is the bloodcurdling scream between my ears.

This is the flashback to me 19 at Dig's Diner where Dig's talking about babysitters and he says We didn't have 'em so other people could raise 'em!

This is the close up on my face and the dramatic music as I realize we will never ever win the lottery.

This is the part where I tell my wife yes, if we win the lottery, we can reverse it.

This is the part where in spite of the last part my wife rages against my machinelike dispassion as I hold a cold Miller High Life against my bruised nuts and then drink from it.

This is the part where the credits roll as the Publisher's Clearing House Prize Patrol rolls into our neighborhood.

These are the people leaving the theatre talking about how the sequel is just too predictable.

I Am a Poet

I am a poet
I don't wear a black turtleneck and beret
to art show openings, slurring the word "actually"
into a glass of red wine and throwing about words
like "aesthetic" and "esoteric" and "vagina"
I prefer writing poetry to talking about it
but just this once I'll do them both at the same time

I am a poet
I'm not a beatnik and I don't want you
to snap your damn fingers after I'm done reading
I believe it is better to have one's idle hands manipulated
by the devil than to play a pair of bongos
I think Jack Kerouac is overrated but Allen Ginsberg is not
I know that it's best to read to a drunken audience
because they may often ignore you, but when they like you,
they really like you

I am a poet
I don't write pot-inspired or LSD-soaked mystical metaphysics
I don't extol the virtues of group sex, especially where group
sexually transmitted disease is involved
I don't woo tender young girls back to my loft and ply them
with burgundy wine, cheap grass and cryptic word hieroglyphics
that all are high-minded code messages for "I'm hurtin' to get laid"
I'm married
I like the legal drugs, I don't care if you smoke cigarettes,
and I don't think Jim Morrison said much worth saying beyond the
pose

I am a poet
I am not obsessed with sex and death
I have the sex drive of a clinically depressed neutered sloth
living in regions of the arctic where it is literally too cold to get a boner
conditioned by renegade naturalists through the use of various audio
and visual stimuli to burp up vomit every time it encounters
a female of its own species that it is not married to
I prefer
to labor under the illusion that those who aren't never were

And that death is a fabrication
propogated by the funeral home industry
and an international cemetery burial plot cartel

I am a poet
That means I submit my work to magazines to be published
I get lots of rejection slips, I also get acceptances
When rejected, I don't rail against the editors who did not choose me
I don't proclaim my misunderstood genius to the world
I don't crack a glass-fragile ego and threaten suicide go on a three-week
bender and come back pretending it was a spiritual experience
Neither do I labor under the pretense that this will bring me
fame and fortune, though truth be told, if it did, I'd take it

I am a poet
I don't know a damn thing about nature
I haven't got a clue about meter
I haven't intentionally rhymed anything since 1983
I don't sell my work to greeting card companies
I don't know anything about the sexual organs of flowering plants
Greek mythology is all Greek to me,
And I had a thesaurus but I burned it in the middle of the night
outside, in a stiff wind
my house almost caught on fire
The moon wasn't even out
There was nothing profound about the experience
But there may be something profound
about this.

Have You Ever Been in Walmart?

Oh, man! Have you ever
been in Walmart and really looked around
at all those people? Simians everywhere.
Cro-Magnons. Half-men half-monkeys.
Cave women with no light in their eyes.
I can't figure out if people go to Walmart
because they're stupid, or if they become
stupid because they go to Walmart. I'm in there
½ hour ago picking up toenail clippers,
a garden hose, the latest Rascal Flatts CD,
an XL T-shirt with a Bugs Bunny University logo,
and a wheel of Sam's Choice liverwurst—you know,
regular Walmart stuff—and I'm waiting
to check out, and it's like I have this cosmic
brain reaction where I can see everybody's IQ
shimmering above their heads like tongues of flame,
and most of 'em are like 72, 74, 63…
and then I have this total paranoid hallucination
that since I came in the sliding doors the Rapture
had begun, only Jesus is this complete intellectual elitist
with meaningless PhDs in Transubstantiation
and Creationist Evolution and Middle Eastern Surrealist Literature,
and all the intelligent people have—poof! you know, gone
above, and somehow I got Left Behind™
with some presidential Antichrist poised to lead an army
of nimrods into genocide of the remaining intelligentsia
so I've got this total intellectual inferiority complex
compounded by the fact that some perverted form of Christianity
is making the Universe go 'round, and then I realize
that I let my medication lapse over a week ago
so I beeline to the pharmacy, begging God
all the while to make my heart stop beating
before drowning in a sea of idiots
like the antihero of a '70s sci-fi movie
starring Charlton Heston as Satan's right hand man.

When I Die

I want my kids to cry
because I want to have been
a good enough dad
that they'd need to

And I want my wife to think, temporarily,
that she could never marry another
not because I don't want her to
but because I want to have been
that good of a husband

I want my friend Oren (not my son Oren, who
will be born in March) to collect all the files
on my computer, and try to get the best work
published

And even if that is vain and futile
which it may well be

I'd still like my friends
to gather together, get good-n-drunk
and take turns reading aloud some of my poems

I hope it doesn't happen
while I'm teaching
because I don't want a memorial service
in the high school gym

And I fear I haven't truly touched enough kids
for very many current or former students to show up

I'd like my wife and kids to be able to remember me,
but also to move on

And if any of my kids are under age 24,
I'd like them to make better choices than I did
at their age

I don't want God or Christ to condemn me

for being a general-issue religious Doubting Thomas
but would hope they'd reward me
for trying to live as a good Catholic
at least ever since I got back into the fold
last Easter

And I know if Allah is running the show
I'm toast, with all the beer I've drunk

Mostly I want to be at peace
and I want to have left things better
than I found them

But also
if anything does manage to get published posthumously
I'd like to read the reviews

About the Author

Steve Henn lives where winter lasts too long. He writes things other than poetry, most of which have not been published. In his spare time, he raises 4 children with Lydia, and grades papers. This is what he has to say about this book: "Sorry, mom." He would like to remind Everyone Involved of the existence of the First Amendment to the Constitution of the United States of America, and of the vital role it plays in the health of the American Democracy. And also of "poetic license," whatever that means. Robert Pollard is his hero. So is Jack Musgrave. And perhaps Phyllis Diller. He is the wickedest wit to come out of Warsaw, Indiana, since Ambrose Bierce.

About NYQ Books™

NYQ Books™ was established in 2009 as an imprint of The New York Quarterly Foundation, Inc. Its mission is to augment the *New York Quarterly* poetry magazine by providing an additional venue for poets already published in the magazine. A lifelong dream of NYQ's founding editor, William Packard, NYQ Books™ has been made possible by both growing foundation support and new technology that was not available during William Packard's lifetime. We are proud to present these books to you and hope that you will continue to support The New York Quarterly Foundation, Inc. and our poets, and that you will enjoy these other titles from NYQ Books™:

Barbara Blatner	*The Still Position*
Amanda J. Bradley	*Hints and Allegations*
rd coleman	*beach tracks*
Joanna Crispi	*Soldier in the Grass*
Ira Joe Fisher	*Songs from an Earlier Century*
Sanford Fraser	*Tourist*
Tony Gloeggler	*The Last Lie*
Ted Jonathan	*Bones & Jokes*
Richard Kostelanetz	*Recircuits*
Iris Lee	*Urban Bird Life*
Michael Montlack	*Cool Limbo*
Kevin Pilkington	*In the Eyes of a Dog*
Jim Reese	*ghost on 3rd*
F. D. Reeve	*The Puzzle Master and Other Poems*
Jackie Sheeler	*Earthquake Came to Harlem*
Jayne Lyn Stahl	*Riding with Destiny*
Shelley Stenhouse	*Impunity*
Tim Suermondt	*Just Beautiful*
Douglas Treem	*Everything so Seriously*
Oren Wagner	*Voluptuous Gloom*
Joe Weil	*The Plumber's Apprentice*
Pui Ying Wong	*Yellow Plum Season*
Fred Yannantuono	*A Boilermaker for the Lady*
Grace Zabriskie	*Poems*

Please visit our website for these and other titles:

www.nyqbooks.org

CPSIA information can be obtained at www.ICGtesting.com
Printed in the USA
LVOW030208231111

256149LV00007B/50/P